FASHION
GREAT DESIGNERS TALKING

FASHION
GREAT DESIGNERS TALKING

BY ANNA HARVEY
DEPUTY EDITOR
BRITISH *VOGUE*

AN INFATUATIONS BOOK

Contents

Foreword

by Anna Harvey

Fashion is the most fickle of Muses, but it is her very capriciousness which has captivated and inspired me. She is a complex figure within whose contradictions are to be found examples of elegance and lack of taste, of clothes that are demure, of sexy clothes, of outlandish creations, of practicality, of wit, and of every material and colour imaginable. Sometimes she is relaxed and informal, but on occasions grand. Often she is available at modest price, but she may demand high prices. If she is one thing to-day, to-morrow she will be another. She is forever re-designing and re-inventing herself, and she will go on doing that. Therein lies my inspiration: the inspiration of change, of elegance and excellence, of humour, of beauty, and of style.

That change is influenced in part by a host of unpredictable factors, but mostly by the brilliance and the skill of the best designers. It is they who, relying upon their own ideas and inspirations, create the clothes, the shoes, the hats that express the style which so much appeals to me. Each garment begins life by being translated from an idea into a sketch. It is with that process of translation that this book is concerned; with that first appearance of the designer's inspiration.

Each contributing designer has, by word or by picture, described his or her own personal inspirations and the philosophies or visions from which those inspirations have developed. What they say provides a rare glimpse of the countless images which make up the best of the fashion world. They are creative artists, and like other artists each has a strong sense of his own individuality. Like other artists, too, each has a keen awareness of the history and traditions of their own art form, and a vision of its future.

There is in the best designers a sense of responsibility, and one can see that in this book. Good designing is not an excuse for self-indulgence. It is the wearing of clothes, but not fashionable clothes, which is a necessity. It is for the fashion designer to produce something which makes that necessity more pleasurable, more fun, more comfortable, more beautiful. Fashion, therefore, ought to be able both to be an art form and to provide a service. A service, moreover, which is available to everyone. The emphasis is, overwhelmingly, on the individual and not the industry. It is the variety of the individuals, in all their shapes and sizes, and with all their preferences, prejudices and infatuations which will provide the continuing inspiration for these designers.

As a *Vogue* editor, I want to provide readers with a comprehensive vision and understanding of fashion at its best. This book does much to demonstrate to the reader why fashion enchants these delights as it does. It is a tribute to the breadth of vision, imagination and inspiration of these designers who go on creating work of excellence. It is a testament, too, to the great range of philosophies from which those inspirations are born.

For me, it is a great pleasure to see my Muse appearing in so many ways.

Anna Harvey

antonio
Berardi

Graduate of Central Saint Martins School of Art and Design, Antonio Berardi financed his first show in 1995 with an overdraft on his credit card and a loan from his parents. Not the standard student production — Manolo Blahnik designed the shoes and Philip Treacy made the hats — the show attracted the interest of the press, and soon Berardi was being pictured in trendy magazines such as *i-D* and *Dazed and Confused*. Having worked with John Galliano, Jasper Conran, Paul Costello and a number of successful Italian companies, Antonio Berardi successfully negotiates the divide between art and commerce.

"I'm not interested in making beautiful things that no one can wear."

ANTONIO BERARDI

Spring/Summer 1997

"A whisper of black chiffon, seamed in the style of seventeenth-century corsetry, finely embroidered in gold thread and caught as if by accident to the left thigh by a fine rouleaux of the same, paid homage to one of the greatest of British illustrative artists, Aubrey Beardsley.
The outfit was topped off with an enormous Beardsleyesque concoction of black organza and velvet petals, painstakingly highlighted with gold leaf by Stephen Jones, and shoes of black stretch netting trimmed with patent leather (reminiscent of fishnet stockings) by Manolo Blahnik.
Glass cabochon rings from Lalique were worn on all fingers, knuckle-duster style, to symbolize both strength and fragility and finally garters of dripping black jet continued the theme.
The look was open to interpretation and so it should be, for fashion should never be an obvious pastiche of things seen before. However the message I wanted to get across was one of today's woman; powerful, sensual yet delicate and at times naive."

MANOLO
BLAHNIK

Manolo Blahnik is a designer acclaimed for his glorious shoes which grace the feet of the likes of Paloma Picasso, Anjelica Huston, Joan Rivers and Winona Ryder. The son of a Czech father and Spanish mother, he grew up in Santa Cruz de la Palma, where he learned about making shoes from watching his mother, who, too impatient to wait for the island cobbler, had taught herself the craft.

"Manolo speaks through his shoes. For him, the foot, the shoe, implies the whole nature of a person, and expresses a story," Italian *Vogue* editor Anna Piaggi.

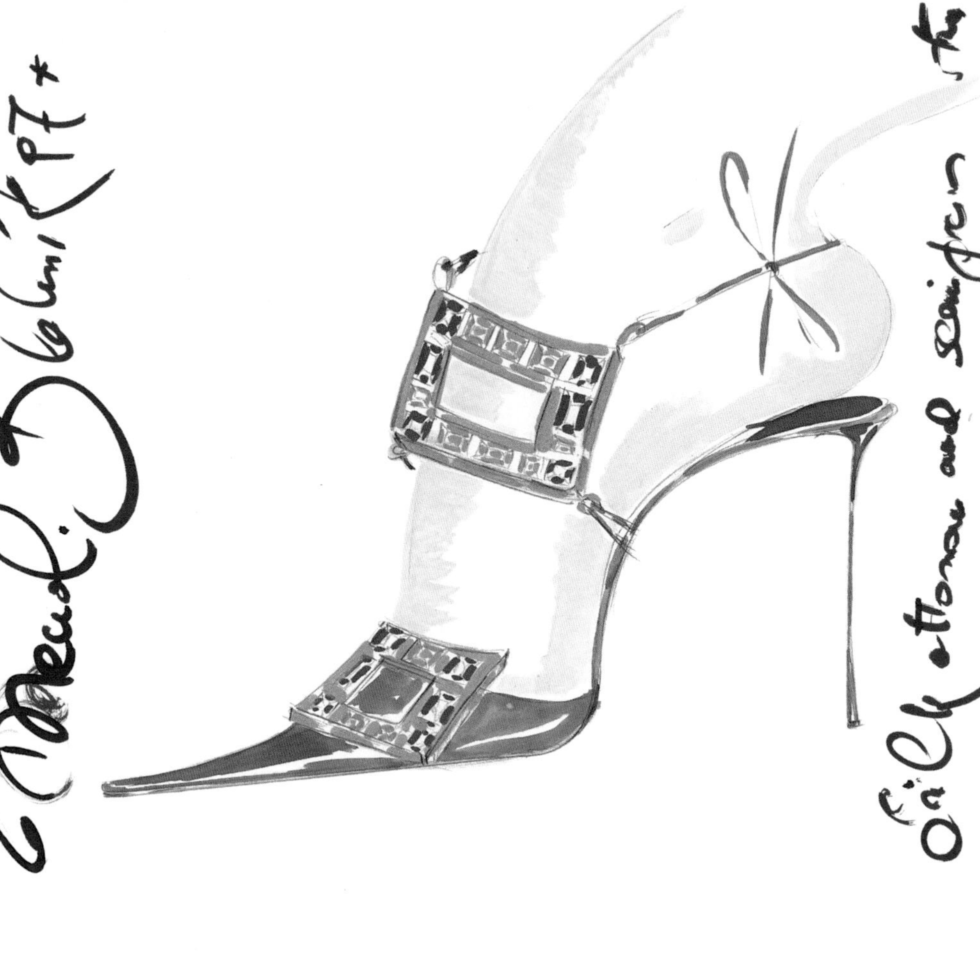

MANOLO BLAHNIK

"These semi-precious stones remind me of Byzance and the

Empress Theodora, the grace and agility of Lisa Fonssagrievs-

Penn, the elegance and gesture of East meets West on the

magnificent movement of Tina Chow...

The essence captured of the past with modernity and attitude

of Linda Evangelista's face.

The southern animalistic fury of Sophia Loren and colours,

smells of churches in Naples and Palermo. The opulent silken

rustle of an ottoman dress in 'The Leopard'".

bill blass

Born in Fort Wayne, Indiana, in 1922, Bill
Blass was one of the first American designer
names to appear on a label. Growing up
during the depression he was bewitched by
the glamourous life that Hollywood portrayed.
He came to New York in 1939 where he
worked first as a sketcher and then as a
designer. Today he is one of the most widely
acclaimed American fashion designers, with
two collections: *Bill Blass Couture* and *Bill
Blass USA*.

"No woman can be well dressed unless she is
comfortable in what she is wearing."

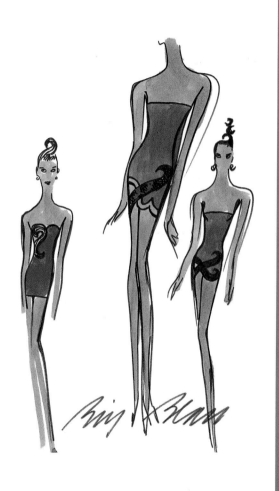

BILL BLASS

"Day clothes are wonderful, but it is the night that truly inspires me. There is always a certain 'uniform' a woman must wear in the day, a definite appropriate look she must have in business, for lunch, for the city, for the country. But at night, there is a wonderful freedom to dressing up. No rules apply.

In the evening, a woman can fantasize and truly explore the many facets of her personality. And, chauvinistic as it may sound, women dress for men at night. Here are two of my favorite — and radically different — ways to dress for evening...long, lean, elegant, sophisticated...short, sexy, bare, hot colors."

Patrick Cox is best known for his modern approach to creating original footwear. Born in Alberta, Canada, he is now based in London. As a student, Patrick Cox created footwear for Vivienne Westwood's Autumn/Winter 1984/5 collection, more recently he has worked with John Galliano, Katharine Hamnett, John Rocha and Jean Colonna. In October 1994 he was named Accessory Designer of the Year at the British Fashion Awards.

Quote on Debbie Harry/Red Slingbacks

"Rock chicks, soul sisters and disco divas are fundamental to my designing. Every season each new group of shoes gets named after one of these amazing babes:- Chaka, Farrah, Siouxie...

These red patent asymmetric slingbacks with towering heels could have been inspired by none other than New Wave icon Debbie Harry. She's so fucking cool!"

Quote on Pee Wee Herman/White "Wannabe" Loafer

"Pee Wee Herman was my hero at the time that I was designing what was to become the 'Wannabe' loafer. His skinny little suits (minus the red bow-tie) were a big inspiration but, it was those white shoes that really caught my eye. I love white shoes on men, they conjure up so many images; senile old golfers in Palm Springs, 'Blaxploitation' pimps in Harlem...ow!

I finally got to meet Pee Wee (Paul Rubens) a couple of years ago and he couldn't believe how a little idea inspired a million pair of shoes. 'Mais oui Pee Wee!'"

DOLCE&GABBANA

Dolce & Gabbana is the trademark of Sicilian Domenico Dolce and Milanese, with Venetian background, Stefano Gabbana. Their designs are famous for their strong Mediterranean influence and discreet sexuality. Sicily is a particularly strong theme in their work, as is a sensuality inspired by the Italian screen heroines of the fifties — women like Anna Magnani and Sophia Loren. After eleven years of activity, Dolce & Gabbana's empire includes boutiques in cities all around the world, including Milan, London, Rome, Paris, Tokyo and New York. In addition to womens wear, their range includes menswear, a women's and men's fragrance, a wide range of accessories, eyewear and the youth line *D & G*. One of their favourite projects is a shop in Milan which is dedicated to the home "because the Dolce & Gabbana style is neither taken off nor put on but lives inside, around and next to the person who looks for and chooses it".

DOLCE & GABBANA

"The exterior vision of an interior world, the visualization of a feeling, the realization of a dream. The imaginary journey to discover one's own roots, the surfacing of memories, perfumes and flavors, never completely forgotten. With ones' own hands creating a world of sentiments that you hold inside and that you would like to give to someone. The passion of the Mediterranean South, so much alive and carnal that it's possible to touch it. The dream interpreted, the construction of tailoring. The sinuousness of the corset, the rigor of the pinstriped suit, the protective wing of a cap and the essentialness of a tank top."

nicole farhi

Born in Nice, Nicole Farhi began her career as a freelance designer in Paris before moving to London in the early 1970s. She launched her first collection in 1983. Her style has since become the epitome of understated, wearable elegance with designs featuring simplicity above fussy-detailing. Nicole Farhi now has both womens and menswear stores in London, as well as shops in Manchester, Oslo and Tokyo. Not driven by the whims of fashion, she attributes her success to consistency in making clothes that last.

NICOLE FARHI

"My philosophy of fashion has always been the same: that there is no reason why the everyday should not be beautiful. For years we were encouraged to think that special clothes belonged to special occasions, but that in our daily lives we should simply make do. On the contrary, I believe that elegance and sophistication can be practical. They can be expressed through clothes that are not just good to look at, but which also make the wearer feel better in herself/himself.

I hate the distinction between the salon and the street. Why should the best and the best made belong only to the a catwalk? Nicole Farhi clothes can be worn at all times of the day and in all kinds of places without any loss of individuality. Refinement need not always be simple, any more than the useful need be ugly. The whole idea of my clothes is that they should be a pleasure to wear. Their impulse is democratic. The shops themselves, I hope, show an easygoing good taste which is relaxed and crucially unself-conscious."

Gianfranco Ferré was born in Italy and graduated in 1969 with a degree in architecture from the Polytechnic Institute of Milan. He surprised everyone by entering the world of fashion, creating jewellery and accessories which were an immediate hit. This success encouraged Ferré to dedicate himself to fashion, a discipline which he saw as anything but frivolous "…an interpretation of contemporary reality that draws inspiration from the rich legacy of the past." Currently Gianfranco Ferré's expanding commercial empire includes both men's and women's lines with 20 clothing collections presented each year, dozens of licences and more than 400 sales outlets worldwide.

GIANFRANCO FERRE

GIANFRANCO FERRE

GIANFRANCO FERRE

GIANFRANCO FERRE

GIANFRANCO FERRE

GIANFRANCO FERRE

"...Colour is an element which right from the initial sketch appears inseparable to me in regard to the idea of the dress, to its substance and nature. My colours are always part of the whole, have a chosen place in the idea from the very first moment of its conception. I have often made reference to the 'Ferré lexicon', that is, the consistent set of signs that connote my style and show up clearly in all my collections. Colours are a natural and fundamental part of this lexicon. And red is it in a really particular way. The 'Ferré red' reveals a character ever true, over time and yet capable of infinite modulations. Season after season distinct tones, specific and necessary, take on unique hues that in turn make up a proper, separate lexicon expressing energy, passion, charm, allure, poetry..."

Alberta **Ferrett**

Born in Italy, Alberta Ferretti learned her trade playing with scraps of fabric in her mother's dressmaker's shop. She opened her first boutique at the age of 18, and in 1974 she designed and produced her first collection, putting into practice all the skills she had learned as a child. Six years later she founded the company Alberta Ferretti, and in 1981 she presented her collection on the catwalks of Milan. There is a harmony between eccentricity and delicacy in her collections, and a very personal style which is reflected in other areas of the designer's life: she has restored and brought back to life the 1920s building in Milan where her company headquarters are based, and has been involved with the restoration of Montegridolfo, a tiny thirteenth- century Medieval village on the border of the Romagna and Marche regions in Italy.

"I am an aesthete who often gets moved; and this is the guiding principle of all my decisions and actions."

ALBERTA FERRETTI

"'Whenever humanity seems condemned to heaviness, I think I should fly like Perseus into a different space...The images of lightness that I seek should not fade away like dreams dissolved by the realities of present and future...'

I must start from my point of arrival, namely 'Le Lezioni Americane', by Italo Calvino, to recount, and perhaps clarify my own thoughts on a strange type of infatuation I have been experiencing for years towards the less definable of sensations: lightness.

Lightness of the fabrics I choose collection after collection.

Lightness in furnishings: desiring only those sensations given by air and light, and some golden and silver flashes.

Lightness in fashion: I soon realized that, subconsciously, I was attempting to create a clean, light silhouette, devoid of stiffness.

While sketching, I had no particular woman in mind — only impressions, flashes, fragments of images. As in the portraits of Cecil Beaton, I found myself designing for women I had admired for their grace, sensibility and lightness: Virginia Wolf, Vanessa Bell, Edith Sitwell, Vita Sackville-West, using that period and those surroundings as the answer to my strongest impulse: to flee from heaviness...

I certainly have intertwined many threads in this conversation. Which one must I pull to reach my conclusion? I prefer the literary aspect which occupies such an important part of our lives. 'We will face the new millennium' writes Calvino, 'with no hope of finding any more than what we ourselves are able to bring to it'.

Hence, I have decided I must be 'light', let go of all the ballast, and bring with me only what I truly care for."

bella
freud

After an early childhood spent travelling in North Africa, Bella Freud was educated in England and then studied fashion at the Academia di Costuma e di Moda in Rome. In 1990 she presented her first collection of knitwear. In this she combined formal tailoring with the restricted sexiness of the Edwardian silhouette to create the provocatively feminine look that she is now famous for. Bella showed her first catwalk collection in Autumn/Winter 1994, and has continued to show in London every season. She has a large clientele in Japan, and loyal customers all over Europe and the USA.

BELLA FREUD
Dress Sense

"Half naked, pondering, filled with gloom,
Though failure may be only hum'n,
'Must extricate myself from this...'
Sartorial Metamorphosis!
Depressive moods and fears must be
Eclipsed by Fashion's Industry.

You may be loved for *just* your shoes.
Your hat — not what you say — is news.
Diogenes knew well that clothes
Triumph o'er poetry and prose.
The certain way to happiness:
Don't change your mind, just change your dress.

One undisputed fact remains:
Inside your wardrobe hang your brains."

Bella Freud
June 1997

ghost

Tanya Sarne is the creative director and business brain behind Ghost. Born in London she spent her early career as a model and later became a teacher. After three years in California with her husband and children, the family travelled through South America and Europe. Arriving back in Britain, Tanya Sarne began importing Peruvian alpaca knits, and her career in fashion began. Her own label *Miz* was launched in 1978, epitomising the casual mood of late seventies fashion. Ghost was launched in 1984, designed by women for women. "...real clothes for real women" each garment is a one off.

GHOST

"Is Fashion an Art? I have asked myself this question many times. Can one compare the most exquisite Dior or Balenciaga creation to a Beethoven sonata, a Botticelli painting or a Shakespeare sonnet. Where is the demand on the intellect? And yet — I argue — it is an Art form. To realise a sketch means to bring it alive with fabric, colour, dimensions, silhouette, cut, fit and something else. Does the art lie in the design or the execution of the design?

The art of fashion for me — is shown by the person who wears it. Fashion gives one the chance to express ones individuality and style. Therein lies the art.

The designer I am working with gave me this sketch to work with. If I were not infatuated with fashion I could not have interpreted these sketches."

LULU GUINNESS

With no formal design training, Lulu Guinness left her job in video production in 1989 and began designing handbags. Her natural talent was quickly recognised and her first design was sold to *Liberty, Joseph* and *Browns* in London. Lulu showed her first full collection in 1990 at the London designer shows, and her work is now sold internationally. Her stockists include *Harrods*, *Harvey Nichols* and *Liberty* in London and *Bergdorf Goodman, Neiman Marcus* and *Saks Fifth Avenue* in the USA. Inspired by old-style glamour, Lulu continues to produce feminine, elegant and beautiful bags.

"A rose is a rose is a rose."

Gertrude Stein

anouska ✳ hempel

Internationally renowned British designer, Anouska Hempel is well known for the diversity and variety of her design projects, from interior and exterior architecturally based designs to couturiere and hotelier. In London her work is best expressed at her hotels, Blakes in South Kensington and The Hempel in Lancaster Gate. Anouska Hempel is noted for her high standards, attention to detail and her personalised style which puts her at the cutting edge of innovation and marks her designs as the lead many follow.

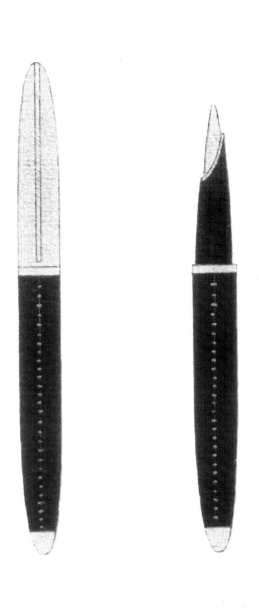

LADY WEINBERG/ANOUSKA HEMPEL
INFATUATIONS — LOUIS VUITTON PENS

"The history and design of pens has been a life long infatuation. A pen allows me total freedom to draw, to write, to use the left-hand part of my brain with punctuation of my right vision, onto paper as my total inspiration and reference. From the papyrus of the early days to the precision of today, it has been a long incredible, indelible journey.

When asked to design my own pen collection for Louis Vuitton, I was extraordinarily flattered and it went beyond infatuation, into obsession! The results are a mixture of detail, perfection and quality in the materials, resulting in an immaculate finish. Unique precision writing instruments, encapsulate the spirit of my travels (and highly likely someone else's) — it whispers to me of shared secrets and adventures yet unknown!

As a designer a pen is the tool of my trade, it is more important to me than a brush stroke. Recording, writing, reasoning and allowing me to relay every journey from the travels of my mind into a total reality is quintessential.

Infatuated, obsessed and the most prized possession that one can have. A tactile, tidy, transference! A pen.

The pen pictured is called Doc. — stitches to the side, as in a Doc. Marten Boot. Street fashion into couture and, as we know a stitch in time saves...everything!"

betty
jackson

Lancashire-born designer Betty Jackson launched her first

collection in 1981 and was given the title of British

Designer of The Year three years later. In 1987 she was

awarded an MBE. She produces two main collections a year,

each complimented by a complete range of accessories.

Other collections include *BJ Accessories*, *BJ Knits*, and *BJ*

Beach. Her designs are sold internationally in leading

fashion stores and in the designer rooms of major

department stores.

BETTY JACKSON

"I always want a quality of Englishness — the decorative, sometimes vaguely eccentric way in which Englishwomen pull different pieces together — and look fabulous."

STEPHAN JANSON

French designer Stephan Janson decided he wanted

to become a Couturier at the age of eight after seeing

a cover featuring Yves Saint Laurent's "Mondrian"

dress. He trained at the Ecole de la Chambre Synicale

de la Haute Couture parisienne and went on to work for

Kenzo, Andrea Odicini and various French

manufacturers. After working as the director of Diane

Von Furstenberg's creative studio for six years he moved

to Milan where he was an immediate success. Some of

his designs were featured in *New York Magazine* where

they caught the eye of the Vice President of *Barneys*. The

New York store became the first account of Stephan

Janson — today his collection can be found in 50 top

stores around the world.

"As a kid, I dreamed of becoming a Couturier.
Very early I realized that to be someone in the Big
Fashion Circus, one had to be able to create a
Revolution. But I also realized that all Revolutions
had been prepared by an Evolution of some sort.
My work is about Evolution.
I enjoy my craft. I enjoy the daily dialogue with the
mystery of fabrics, the game of colour combinations,
the long lasting pleasure of well made clothes, the
respect of a woman's body and soul.
The only reward I care for is the faithfulness of
my clients.
In Fashion, as in Life, it takes a long time for a new
vision to be accepted.
In Fashion, as in Life, I prefer whispers to screams."

joseph

Born in Casablanca, Joseph Ettedgui initially trained as a hairdresser and had his own salon on the King's Road in Chelsea during the swinging sixties. He began to display clothing in his salon, and soon established his own shop. He now has numerous shops in London, two in New York, five in Paris and one in Cannes. While he has always retailed other designers, over the last decade Joseph has built up a line of his own which he sells in his stores.

Joseph on his favourite piece from the Autumn/Winter 97/98 Collection:

"I always like to mix different ideas to see what little surprises come out of them. I am spontaneous but I don't let impulse take over from instinct. I always have to have a right feeling for everything I do. This crêpe smoking suit is probably one of my favourite things this season because it has the overall feeling of what this Collection is about. I adore the simplicity, the masculine cut gives such a pure and clean definition. The trousers are strongly influenced by classic men's tailoring but with the soft crêpe fabric they become instantly elegant and very sexy. I love the confidence that this combination brings to the suit."

DONNA KARAN

Born on Long Island, New York, Donna Karan was surrounded by the world of fashion from an early age: her father was a haberdasher and her mother was a showroom model and fashion sales representative. Her first collection was designed and produced for a fashion show while she was still at high school. Straight from fashion school, Donna Karan went to work for Anne Klein, and was named successor after her death in 1974. Ten years later she set up her own company which has since grown to include hosiery, shoes, underwear, eyewear, belts and jewellery. menswear, childrens wear and beauty products.

"The inspiration and creative energy for these devoré dresses came from an all-embracing feeling for the body, art, fashion and fabric."

Lainey
Keogh

Dublin-based knitwear designer Lainey Keogh never studied art or fashion, instead she trained in microbiology and went on to work in a hospital laboratory. She began knitting when she fell in love, and wanted to create a special item of clothing for her boyfriend. Although the relationship didn't last, her passion for knitwear did, and she soon began to receive commissions from friends. In 1994 she was asked to produce some pieces for designer Michael Mortell for his Autumn/Winter collection. Lainey Keogh's soft, sensual pieces are all hand-crafted in Ireland, and are worn by celebrities including Elizabeth Taylor, Demi Moore, the Stones, Jack Nicholson and Whoopi Goldberg.

"She is Dakini,

Skydancer,

She who floats freely

Woman,

Beautiful,

Divine inspiration."

CHRIS
TIANLA
CROIX

Christian Lacroix grew up in the south of France. As a child he was fascinated by the traditions of Provence, the theatre and opera, art galleries, old books and photographs. He took an arts degree at the University of Montpellier and went on to the Sorbonne and the Ecole du Louvre in Paris, intending to become a museum curator. In Paris he met people who encouraged him to design, and his career flourished. In 1987 he was awarded the title of most influential foreign designer by the CFDA in New York, and, joining forces with Jean-Jacques Picart and Bernard Arnault, the House of Christian Lacroix was founded. In addition to his collections Haute-Couture, casual wear, accessories, perfume and household textiles, Christian Lacroix has retained a passion for the theatre, designing for a number of productions. These include *Phèdre* for which he was awarded by the "Molière" (French Theatre Awards) for best costumes.

"Fashion for me is really not looking

like your neighbour but to resemble

yourself and in order to allow each

woman to freely express her

individuality I try to sketch the future

by mixing past and present, space and

time, combining historical styles and

ethnic influences, all of this with

today's impulse, rhythm and modernity,

may they come from music, sports or

the street."

RALPH LAUREN

Born in New York, Ralph Lauren introduced Polo neckwear in 1967 — his work has since come to symbolise the best of American design. The first *Polo* store was opened in Beverly Hills in 1971, and there are now 100 *Polo/Ralph Lauren* stores around the world. Currently his range includes men's women's and children's clothing, accessories, home furnishings and fragrances all of which are inspired by a combination of romance, tradition and innovation.

"Everything I do has a personal reference, a personal sensibility. I feel it, it's who I am."

"My theory about clothes for men and women is that it's about a person, an image, a concept. It's style, not fashion."

julien
macdonald

Brought up in the Welsh Valleys, Julien MacDonald had already contributed to the collections of several top designers before leaving college in 1996. His graduation collection caught the eye of Karl Lagerfeld, and Julien moved to Paris to work for Chanel, where within two weeks he was appointed knitwear designer for Chanel ready-to wear. He followed this up with his well-received first show, "Mermaids", staged during London Fashion Week.

MERMAIDS
JULIEN MACDONALD

"Once upon a time, I imagine it was at the turn of the century...

A beautiful young orphan boy is cast adrift in a ship with his governess. Throughout the voyage the boy never glimpses the sea. The governess keeps him down below in a tiny cabin where she teaches him Latin and algebra, all the time dressed in a stiff dress that is as mysterious as the night.

When the ship anchors six months later in Capri, the boy is lowered into a small wooden boat. His first sight of the sea is extraordinary: the water is frozen and a delicate white mist hovers above it. The orphan discovers a tiny hole in the bottom of the boat. He wriggles through it and finds himself in a magical place, another world where the water is the colour of crystal and the rocks are glinting with a strange, dark sparkle. Fish flash around him and he realised something has become entangled in his net. It is a mermaid. Her locks of hair swirl around her face and tumble right down to her silvery tail which glints in the dark: she sings mysterious songs of the sea and sailors. She silently pulls him from the watery depth: the net is covered by a magical frost of jewels and vibrant colours.

Back on the ship, the boy never forgets the mermaid. Secretly every night, by candlelight, he makes dresses for the little mermaid. They are made from the magical threads of the fishing net. They are magical dresses..."

ALEXANDER
MCQUEEN

London born and educated designer Alexander McQueen has been dubbed "enfant terrible" by the fashion press. In 1996 he became one of the youngest to achieve the title Designer of the Year. He learned the skills of pattern-making working for several Saville Row tailors, including Bermans and Nathans, the famous theatrical costumers. At the age of 20 he was employed by the innovative Japanese designer Koji Tatsuno, before travelling to Milan where he worked with Romeo Gigli. Returning to London he completed an M.A at St. Martins School of Art where his final collection caught the attention of *Vogue* editor Isabella Blow, with this his reputation was established and his meteoric rise to success ensured.

"I am myself when I am flying the falcons, being on my own with nature is so relaxing, I can let my mind go, allowing ideas for the collections to develop."

ISAAC M

Born and brought up in New York, Isaac Mizrahi began his career in fashi
graduation from Parsons School of Design he was apprenticed to Perry E
as Jeffrey Banks and Calvin Klein before opening his own business with
Avenue's Darling", Isaac Mizrahi has twice been awarded the coveted CF
are renown for their classical simplicity. "I have always believed that sim
roots of what is truly American — clothes that are pared down, comforta

IZRAHI

ge of 13 designing clothes for his mother's friends. Following his
n he calls his "guardian angel". He went on to work with designers such
ad-Cheney. Lauded as "the Wonder Boy", the "Whiz Kid" and "Seventh
r of the Year Award, once in 1990 and again two years later. His designs
essential part of American design", he states "..I try to reach the tap
tical, yet have a sense of luxury and an element of wit and surprise."

"These clothes to me are like good architecture. The details are as important to the shape as the shapes themselves. The focus of these clothes is on design — and they become fashion only when worn — the woman gives them personality."

ISAAC MIZRAHI
APRIL 1997

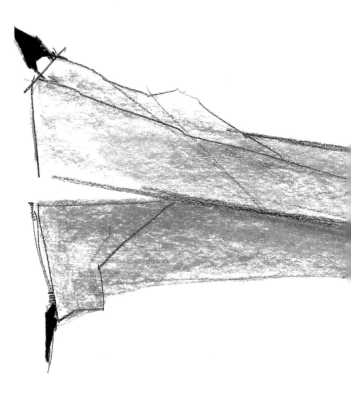

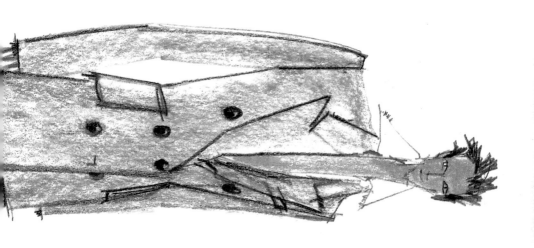

RED OR
DEAD

Wayne and Geraldine Hemingway created Red or Dead with a small market stall in Camden, London — the label now receives global recognition for its distinctive footwear, clothing and accessories. The company was acquired by the Penland Group plc in June 1996 although the Hemingways still retain their creative capacity. Currently with seven outlets in the UK and franchises overseas, the aim of Red or Dead remains "To produce innovative, challenging fashion at affordable prices and on a non-elitist level". The name Red or Dead originated as a proud reference to Wayne Hemingway's ancestry. His father is Billy Two Rivers, a Mohawk Indian chief who is now a politician heading a council of Indian chiefs for the Kawanake tribe in Quebec, Canada.

RED OR DEAD

"Red or Dead has always had a vision to be the first designer label that catered for, and could be afforded by, an increasing number of young people who were growing up with style and being fed design information by an explosion of media coverage, but who could not afford the high prices that traditionally went hand in hand with designer labels. This concept that was widely considered to be inappropriate in the power mad eighties has been widely accepted and applauded in the 90s. By continuing British irony, irreverence, youthful creativity and accessibility we have brought something new to the fashion world — Designer Street Fashion."

SONIA **RYKIEL**

Recognised as the undisputed "Queen of Knitwear", Sonia Rykiel created her first maternity dresses and body-hugging sweaters for the Paris boutique *Laura* in 1962. She went on to launch her own company, Sonia Rykiel CDM, six years later.

"She invents fashion from one day to the next.

She loves the everyday and the decorative, theatre, poetry, literature, painting and the family.

Attentive to the world and a witness to what happens in it. She loves clothes that go together, that play together, that are organized together but also clothes that shine and sparkle. She likes to put seams inside out, take away the hem and the lining, and then, if she wants, to put it all as it was before.

She loves writing.

She writes on her sweaters, her belts and her bags.

She loves accessories.

She loves 'nourishment', and nourishes her clothes as well."

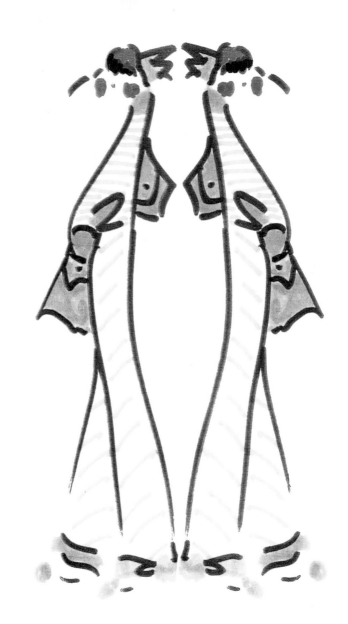

Sonia Rykiel

"Femme Humour, femme Sculpture, femme Scandale, femme Drôle, femme Double.

Femme redessinée, travaillée, femme pas naturelle, femme jeu.

Femme émotion, femme collection. Femme départ, femme floue, femme fragile.

Femme à l'envers, puis à l'endroit.

Femme fil ou femme maille.

Femmes, je vous aime."

JIL SA

The best-known German fashion designer, Jil Sander has built her fashion empire around impeccably crafted minimalist clothes, cosmetics and perfumes. In 1968 she sold her car to finance her first store in Hamburg, and four years later launched the first full Jil Sander collection. She currently has six company-owned stores, 19 franchises around the world and Jil Sander shops in both *Harrods* and *Browns* of South Molton Street, London.

JIL SANDER

**"THE INNER SPACE IS
SEEN BY PEERING THROUGH THE
EYE"**

Paul **Smith**

Paul Smith's introduction into the world of fashion was completely accidental. At 18, with no qualifications or career direction, his father marched him off to the local clothing warehouse where he was employed as a "gofer". His interest in fashion developed and in 1970 at the age of 24 he opened his own shop — and the business grew. Paul Smith's first collection was shown in Paris in 1976. Today there are Paul Smith shops in London, Manchester, Nottingham, New York, Hong Kong, Singapore, Bangkok, Taipei, Jakarta, Seoul and Japan. In 1994 he was awarded a CBE for services to the fashion industry.

PAUL SMITH

"I have chosen an outfit from my Spring/Summer 1993 'Dandy meets Rock & Roll' collection which pioneered the now ubiquitous, slimmer silhouette and more flamboyant look for men. At the time it caused quite a stir — close fitting shirts with long collars and lace cuffs, tight lurex t-shirts and sharply tailored, fitted suits with cigarette trousers were in complete contrast to the, then, trend for looser, easier shapes. It was a very exciting time. Ironically, I'm having as much fun now designing easier, looser suits with very wide trousers for Spring/Summer 1998 although the now 'classic' slim fit suit continues...in red silk devoré — very Dandy meets rock and roll."

VALE

Valentino Garavani was born in Voghera in Italy. In the 1950s as a young man he moved to Paris to study fashion design. Apprenticed to Jean Dessès and Guy Laroche, he developed his own style which, on his return to Italy, made him one of his country's top designers. His first show was held in 1962 at the Pitti Palace in Florence, where he was received enthusiastically by the international fashion press.

One of the most significant moments of Valentino's career

TINO

came with the appointment of Giancarlo Giammetti as his business partner, under whose influence the commercial and economic growth of the company has been assured. In a career spanning four decades, Valentino's influence on the fashion world has been considerable, and with his motto "Creation and Elegance" he has dressed some of the world's most famous women, including Jacqueline Kennedy and Elizabeth Taylor.

MR VALENTINO

"When I create, I always try to express a 'timeless' elegance. It is not a disposable six month fantasy, quite the contrary, something that defines fashion in time.

I always address the elegance, femininity and romance of women when I design, that is very much my signature and trademark, I know that

I am very much known for that.

I get inspired by people, music, films, my own homes, travelling, the streets of London, Paris or

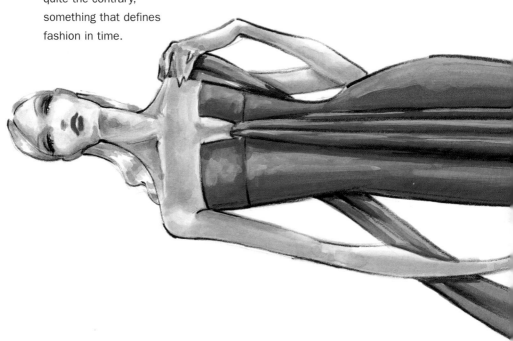

New York. Great energy coming from meeting new and fun people, attending a great event, anything and everything feeds me in one way or another.

Regarding beauty, the character and personality of the modern woman are far more interesting, challenging and seductive than plain beauty. Of course, all three combined are the most seductive package you can have! But, modernity today is most certainly defined by character: intelligent, articulate and outspoken women, comfortable in their own minds and skin, are to me incredibly sexy."

GIANNI **VERSACE**

Gianni Versace was born in Italy in 1946. At the age of 25 he moved to Milan and began working for the top fashion houses of the time, the first women's collection to carry his name was shown in 1978. He won the first of the many awards that were to punctuate his career — 'L'Occhio d'Oro (The Golden Eye) — in 1982, the same year that he began to work with La Scala Theatre, designing costumes for *Josephlegende*. Versace's range of collections includes clothing, jewellery, watches, perfumes, accessories and homewear. In 1993 he was awarded the much coveted American Fashion Oscar by the Council of Fashion Designers of America.

The tragic death of Gianni Versace in 1997 was a profound loss to the world of fashion, where his creative influence is greatly missed.

GIANNI VERSACE

..ART..
...LOVE...
....BEAUTY....
.....FASHION.....
......CURIOSITY......
.......FRIENDSHIP.......
....................TRAVELLING....................
...........MOVIES...........
......NATURE......
.....FAMILY.....
....MUSIC.....
...BOOKS...
..SEX..

and many, many other INFATUATIONS are the great part of my LIFE

GEORGINA
VON ETZDORF

Georgina von Etzdorf is the signature of a range of distinctive hand-printed accessories, fabric and clothing. The founders of the company — Georgina von Etzdorf, Martin Simcock and Jonathan Docherty — met at art school in the seventies, and are motivated by designing and manufacturing innovative products of the finest quality. The company has recently launched an interiors collection, incorporating cushions, throws, bolsters and bean bags to accompany its already highly established scarf and clothing lines.

"JUPITER" (1987) by Georgina von Etzdorf

"With a passion for colour and texture, the company has always tried to fuse artistry with production. This initial sketch, for the scarf design 'Jupiter', launched our experiments with our own hand screen printing to interpret three-dimensional layering and water colour effects on fabric. This marked a thrilling turning point in our approach to textile design."

AMANDA **WAKELEY**

Amanda Wakeley launched her own label four years ago at the age of 29 — two years later she opened her own shop in London's Fulham Road. With key stockists such as *Harvey Nichols* and *Harrods*, she now produces two collections a year. Her designs are uncomplicated, modern and understated — intended to appeal to the customer rather than the press. Amanda Wakeley has won three British Fashion Awards for Glamour in 1992, 1993 and 1996 and is now firmly established as one of the UK's leading designers.

AMANDA WAKELEY

"Basing myself in London ensures a vital atmosphere in which to live and work. It's a city with a passion for life and has a constantly shifting cultural landscape which absorbs ideas from the street to the very high brow. This has a self perpetuating effect on the creation of new ideas. It's a city that knows how to party, sometimes to its detriment, but I love the energy here.

In contrast, I spend part of my time aboard my boat moored off France's graceful south coast. Its turquoise waters and warm sun instill a feeling of well being.

I believe in aiming for the highest quality of life possible. This sentiment is carried through into all areas of my life and into my work. I design each collection using luxury cloths and fine cashmeres that feel fantastic next to the skin. The cut of the garment is also designed to feel sexy and make the woman feel confident. If I can help a woman feel good about herself, then I have succeeded as a designer."

VIVIENNE
WESTWOOD

Born in Glossop, Derbyshire, Vivienne Westwood moved to London with her family when she was 17. She began designing in 1971 using her shop in King's Road, London as a showcase. Initially known as *Let it Rock* it sold 1950's Rock 'n' Roll records and clothing, it became *Too Fast to Live, too Young to Die* a year later and began stocking clothes for "Rockers" with zips and chains — the name and stock of the shop changed several more times to reflect evolving ideas. Vivienne Westwood's first collection was shown in March 1981, and in 1983 she became the first British designer since Mary Quant to show in Paris. Today Vivienne Westwood Ltd. is a company with four labels: *Vivienne Westwood Gold Label*, for which many garments are made to measure following the tradition of haute couture; *The Red Label by Vivienne Westwood*, made in Italy; *Man*, Vivienne Westwood's mens line launched in 1996 and *Anglomania*, launched in 1997 which includes re-workings of some favourite pieces from past collections.

Costume in grey flannel with bordeau borders which are integral to the fabric: the "look of the collection", Five Centuries Ago (Autumn/Winter 1997/98) inspired by designs of the sixteenth century. Sketch by Andreas Kronthaler.

VIVIENNE WESTWOOD

"As a fashion designer, costume archives and picture galleries are essential to my work; Ideas depend on maintaining the links with tradition.

It's so much to do with seeing the originality of *things in themselves*. You have to be able to recognise originality in order to abstract from it what you need. This is the process often referred to as inspiration.

Unfortunately, in the age of Me, me, me! people see only themselves in everything. The resulting cliché amounts to a veto on ideas.

Orthodoxy is the grave of intelligence. Today we have no avant-garde like the one in nineteenth-century France which rejected the stagnation of official and academic views. We live under a tyranny of orthodox beliefs which threatens us with another Dark Age.

Perhaps our worst orthodoxy is the notion of 'modernity' when this concept is used to discredit the past. This is a false idea which undermines true progress. Since about 1910 history has been denounced *en bloc*, exemplified in Henry Ford's silly dictum 'History is Bunk'. Then, in all fields of applied art, a mania for minimalism' and extreme simplicity became established. However this over-simplification is usually only the fear of committing bad taste. I prefer to allow some choice, and rely on the *chic* of the wearer."

WORKE
FREE

Designer Richard Nott and manager/administrator Graham Fraser formed Workers for Freedom in October 1985. The company was created to enable Nott and Fraser to move away from the constraints of high-profile positions within the fashion industry and to allow them to work towards their own vision of "Freedom of expression". Voted British Designer of the Year in

RS FOR

DOM

1990, Workers for Freedom have a number of celebrity devotees, including Diana Ross, Jamie Lee Curtis and Vanessa Redgrave. During the 1990s they have shifted their focus away from retail and have undertaken various consultancy projects as well as developing and designing ranges of womenswear, menswear and shoes for *Littlewoods Home Shopping*.

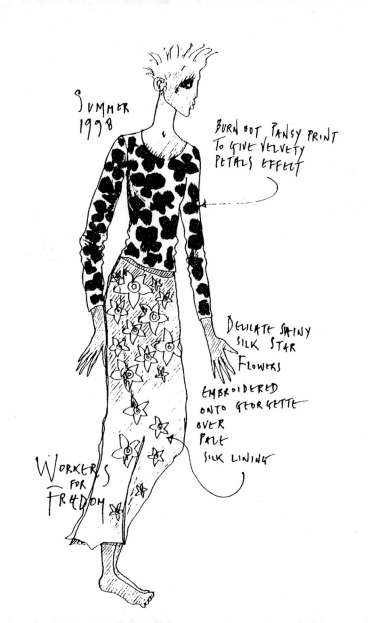

SUMMER 1998

BURNOUT PANSY PRINT TO GIVE VELVETY PETALS EFFECT

DELICATE SHINY SILK STAR FLOWERS EMBROIDERED ONTO GEORGETTE OVER PALE SILK LINING

WORKERS FOR FREEDOM

WORKERS FOR FREEDOM

"A new collection, the ideas glimmer in the back of the mind,
distant stars in a hazy sky off to Santa Fe, again? The frenzy
of India? Black and white?
Perhaps, perhaps..... but like a growing itch they force their
way into the picture like wood anemones through the dead
leaves of winter
inevitable, impossible to ignore, impossible to capture
the colour, the delicacy
the strength and the fragility
the light through the petals
the ruffling breeze
the smell, the surprise

the work begins
the huge oily ugly machines, the bits of cloth, miles of sewing
thread
big cold scissors, the rejects on the factory floor......

Again, here we are, trying to satisfy our infatuation......

The extraordinary and endless beauty of FLOWERS"

Thank you

What excites a designer to create collections which re-invent the human form and inspire us to look at ourselves with fresh eyes? This was the question I discussed with Anna Harvey, Deputy Editor of British *Vogue*. Out of that discussion came *FASHION – great designers talking*.

In a fundamental sense this is Anna's book. It was Anna who spoke to the extraordinary designers represented here, and she who encouraged them to express in words and images what it is that inspires, encourages and drives them to create.

Preparing this book for publication was a delight. We owe many, many thanks to Anna Harvey and her marvellous staff at British *Vogue*, especially Gaia Geddes. Finally, to all the fashion designers who contributed to this book, we say thank you – and hope that *FASHION* will prove a treasured source of inspiration for the rest of us.

Susan Jenkins

MQ Publications

Directory

Antonio Berardi
59 St Martin Lane
St Martin's House
London WC2

Manolo Blahnik
49-51 Old Church Street
London SW3 5BS, UK
tel: 0171 352 8622
fax: 0171 351 7314

Bill Blass
Bill Blass Ltd
550 Seventh Avenue
New York, New York 10018
tel: 212 221 6660
fax: 212 398 5545

Patrick Cox
Press Department
30 Sloane Street
London SW1X 9NJ, UK
tel: 0171 235 5599

Dolce & Gabbana
Dolce & Gabbana Press Office
Via Santa Cecilia, 7
20122 Milan, Italy
tel: 39 2 7601 3232
fax: 39 2 7602 0600

Nicole Farhi
158 New Bond Street
London W1, UK

Gianfranco Ferré
Gianfranco Ferre' SpA
Via Sant' Andrea, 18
20121 Milan, Italy
tel: 39 2 784 460
fax: 39 2 781 485

Alberta Ferretti
Via Donizetti, 48
20122 Milan, Italy
tel: 02 760591
fax: 02 782373

Bella Freud
Freud Studio
48 Rawstorne Street
London E14 7ND
tel: 0171 7136466

Ghost
The Chapel
263 Kensal Road
London W10 5DB, UK
tel: 0181 969 1264

Lulu Guinness
66 Ledbury Road
London W11 2AJ, UK
tel: 0171 221 9686
fax: 0171 243 221167

Anouska Hempel
Blakes
33 Roland Gardens
London SW7 3PF, UK
tel: 0171 370 6701
fax: 0171 3730442

Betty Jackson
Brian Morel PR
Heddon House
149/151 Regents Street
London W1R 7LA, UK

Stephan Janson
c/o Apolide
Via P. Calvi 30
20129 Milan, Italy
tel: 55 19 3855
fax: 55 19 3839

Joseph
Press Office
74 Sloane Avenue
London SW3 3DZ, UK
tel: 0171 590 6200
fax: 0171 584 3984

Donna Karan
tel: 001 212 789 1500

Lainey Keogh
Marianne Gunn O'Connor
24 South Anne Street
Dublin 2, Eire
tel: 00 353 16793 299

Christian Lacroix
Press Office
73 rue du Faubourg Saint-Honoré
75008 Paris, France
tel: 01 42 68 79 05
fax: 01 42 68 79 51

Ralph Lauren
143 New Bond Street
London W1Y 9FD, UK
tel: 0171 493 4828
fax: 0171 499 0887

Julien MacDonald
tel: Karen Maher on 0973 886779

Alexander McQueen
58-60 Rivington Street
London EC2A 3PJ, UK

Isaac Mizrahi
104 Wooster Street
New York, NY 10012, USA

Red or Dead
Red Rooster PR
Levels 1 & 2
D'Arblay House
10a Poland Street
Soho
London W1V 3DE, UK
tel: 0171 494 11383
fax: 0171 2887 0693

Sonia Rykiel
175 Boulevard Saint-Germain
75006, Paris, France
tel: 01 49 54 60 60

Jil Sander
Press Office
Osterfeldstrasse 32-34
22529 Hamburg, Germany
tel: 0049 40 55 3020
fax: 0049 40 55 330 34

Paul Smith
Paul Smith Limited
40-41 Floral Street
London WC2E 9DJ, UK
tel: 0171 836 7828

Valentino
Valentio S.p.A.
Piazza Mignanelli 22
00187 Rome, Italy

Gianni Versace
Atelier Gianni Versace
Via Gesù N.12
Milan 20121, Italy
tel: 0276031

Georgina von Etzdorf
31a Sloane Street
London SW1X 9NR, UK
0171 245 1066

Amanda Wakeley
80 Fulham Road
London SW3 6HR, UK
tel: 0171 584 4009

Vivienne Westwood
Press Office
44 Conduit Street
London W1R 9FB, UK
tel: 0171 287 3188
fax: 0171 437 2203

Workers For Freedom
c/o Palladio Associates
6-10 Lexington street
London W1R 3HS, UK
tel: 0171 734 0123
fax: o171 287 0526

Published by MQ Publications Limited
254-258 Goswell Road, London EC1V 7EB

© MQ Publications Limited 1998

ISBN: 1-897954-04-2

Designed by Senate

Printed and bound in Italy

ACKNOWLEDGMENTS:

MQ Publications extend their thanks to all the designers included in this book.
The copyright for all images and photographs remains with the designers
unless otherwise stated.

Photograph of Anna Harvey on page 5 © Lord Snowdon
Photograph of Deborah Harry on page 22 © Brian Aris
Photograph on page 30 © Mikael Jansson
Illustration on page 46 © Susanne Deeken
Photograph on page 58 © Chris Moore
Illustration on page 74 © Romio Shresta
Photographs on page 86 © Sean Ellis
Photograph of Alexander McQueen on page 90 © Chris Moore
Text and images on pages 102/3 © Sonia Rykiel
Photograph of Linda Evangelista on page 106 Peter Lindbergh
Illustration on page 110 © Paul Smith Limited
Illustration on page 130 © Vivienne Westwood Limited